Jonah and the Whale

This

Bible Story Time book

belongs to

_____

_____

_____

Text by Sophie Piper
Illustrations copyright © 2005 Estelle Corke
This edition copyright © 2014 Lion Hudson

Published by Lion Children's Books
an imprint of
Lion Hudson plc
Wilkinson House, Jordan Hill Road,
Oxford OX2 8DR, England
www.lionhudson.com/lionchildrens

ISBN 978 0 7459 6358 7
e-ISBN 978 0 7459 6811 7

First edition 2005
This edition 2014

A catalogue record for this book is available from the British Library

Printed and bound in China, October 2014, LH06

Bible Story Time

Jonah and the Whale

Sophie Piper * Estelle Corke

LION
CHILDREN'S

Jonah was a prophet. When God spoke, Jonah listened. Then he told other people God's message.

One particular day, God asked Jonah to do something.

"Go to Nineveh. The people there do wicked things. Tell them I've noticed how bad they are."

Jonah frowned. "Hmph," he said. "The people of Nineveh are our enemies."

8

"In fact," he said to himself, "I won't go."

Jonah knew which road led to Nineveh. He went the other way, to a town called Joppa.

Down by the harbour was a boat. It was ready to sail to Spain.

"I'll go there!" said Jonah.

He paid his fare and climbed on board.

That night, a storm blew up.

"RRAAHH," roared the wind.

"CRRRASSHH," went the waves.

"Help! We're sinking," cried the sailors. "Help! Help!"

The captain found Jonah asleep.

"Get up and pray!" he ordered. "Ask your god to save us."

The sailors were all praying, but the storm grew worse.

"A powerful god is angry with one of us," said a sailor. "Let's do the choosing game to find out who."

It was Jonah.

"I'm sorry," he said. "I'm running away from God. You'll have to throw me overboard."

The sailors tried to row the ship to shore, but it was no good.

They shouted to heaven. "O God, whoever you are, we're really sorry. Please don't blame us!"

Then they picked Jonah up and threw him into the sea.

Splash!

The little ship sailed safely away.
Jonah sank deep down among the
seaweed and the fishes.
Then...

gulp

"Oh," said Jonah. "I thought that was the end of me. But suddenly everything has changed.

"I think I've been swallowed by a most enormous fish.

"It must be a miracle. Well… in that case, I'd better say a prayer."

He began.

"Thank you, God, for saving me. I'm very sorry. Please keep me alive, and then I'll do what you want."

He waited and waited and waited. Then he felt himself being thrown forward.

"Help!" he began.

The fish spat Jonah onto a beach.

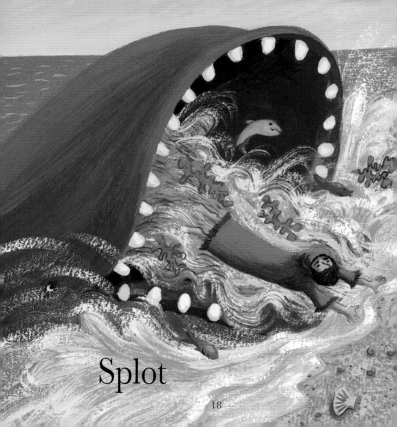

Splot

Jonah went straight to Nineveh.
"Listen up, you Ninevites!" cried
Jonah. "God says this: you have
been very wicked. In forty days,
God will destroy your city."

"Oh my!" said the people of
Nineveh. "Oh dear! Oh no! Oh
help!"

The king of Nineveh called all the people together.

"Listen everyone," he announced. "We must show God we are sorry.

"No one is to eat anything. Everyone is to wear scratchy sackcloth. All of us must pray to God.

"Most of all, we must stop doing wicked things. Then, perhaps, God will forgive us."

"I'm pleased," said God. "I think I'll forgive them."

Jonah heard what God said and it made him angry.

"I knew it, God," he said. "That's what I was afraid you'd do."

Jonah stomped out of the city.

He found a place to sit. He wanted to watch what happened next.

23

The sun shone brightly.

"Phew, it's hot here," he said to himself. "I need to make a shelter."

He worked all day. The shelter was good, but Jonah was still hot.

"I wish there was some shade," he said. "Oh… look at that plant! It's growing before my very eyes."

Jonah watched as the plant grew round his shelter. He watched the leaves unfold. They were huge and gave lovely cool shade.

"This is very nice," said Jonah. "Perhaps things aren't so bad after all."

The next day, Jonah heard a sound.

Munch,

munch,

munch!

A worm came and chewed the stem and the leaves. Very soon, the plant died.

"My poor plant!" cried Jonah. "Now I'll have no shade when the sun gets hot."

The day grew hotter and hotter.
"It's horrible out here," said Jonah.
"I wish I were dead."

Then he heard God speaking.

"Why are you angry about the plant, Jonah?

"I was the one who made it grow for you. You did nothing. Yet you feel sorry for it."

"I do indeed!" said Jonah.

"I made the people of Nineveh," said God. "There are thousands of them. Grown ups, children – and all their animals. I feel sorry for them. That is why I am going to forgive them."